ILLUSTRATIONS BY
NES VUCKOVIC

EVERYDAY
MAGIC

RITUALS, SPELLS & POTIONS
TO LIVE YOUR BEST LIFE

SEMRA HAKSEVER

hardie grant books

ACTION
+
INTENTION
=
MAGIC

CONTENTS

WELCOME TO MY BOOK!

My journey leading up to embracing my inner witch has been varied, with a common thread of being in the business of making people feel good!

For a decade I worked as a freelance fashion stylist, then I spent two years studying for a psychology degree, but dropped out – it was waaaay too much maths and rats and stats for a spiritual soul such as myself. I then ran away with the circus (kind of!), when I spent a few summers travelling around in a motorhome named Destiny, performing an immersive comedy show with my best friend.

I have always been interested in all things metaphysical; aware of synchronicities as signs from the universe, tuning in to my intuition and feeling very connected to the power of the moon.

Then a synchronicity that has had a huge impact on my life happened when I found a book on scent magic at a car boot sale. I got hooked on learning about how scents are used in spells as an offering to the spirits. It was, as Oprah Winfrey would say, my 'Aha!' moment.

I geeked out learning about the magical properties of herbs, plants, flowers, stems, seeds, roots and oils – all gifts from Mother Earth, which when blended and burned send out powerful signals that are released into the universe.

Adding to their power is also recognising that they have been used in sacred ceremonies for thousands of years. To think that cinnamon was used to bless temples in ancient China, that the Egyptians were burning frankincense and myrrh as offerings to the deities, and that witches were using camphor and thyme to consecrate their tools totally blows my mind. I often wonder what energy and magic we would be able to harness today if magic had continued to be practised so widely until now. I highly recommend considering a plant's lineage to help you focus on how much magical history and how many superpowers it contains while you are making your own magical blends.

I really embrace the ethos of feelgood magic and I truly believe in the power of spreading cosmic vibrations.

I hope that these spells and rituals empower you as they have me.

HEALING

WISE

KNOWING

MEDICINAL

NATURAL

THE HISTORY OF MAGIC

Thousands of years ago, witches were known as healers; they were looked upon as the wise men and women of the community, carrying a deep knowledge of both magical and medicinal components of plants and possessing a strong connection to animals. They were the medical practitioners of their time, working closely with nature's cycles and honouring the changing of seasons.

Rituals were practised for healing, protection, warding off evil, reversing curses and attracting good fortune and love. These witches also experimented with hypnosis and astral projection through raising their own consciousness and spiritual ability, which allowed them to work with magical rites in order to have psychic insights and visions into the future.

In these times, if you went to see a witch for an illness they would prepare for you a healing blend of herbs to improve your health, as well as write you a spell to go with it for protection, to prevent further sickness. It is interesting to see that many of the plants and herbs that were recorded as being used to cure illnesses by these witches were also noted as being used to banish negative energy. At the time, such expertise and knowledge was a huge threat to the new religion of Christianity – to think that magic could change the course of someone's will would have suggested that there was something out there that was greater than God.

HOW TO USE THIS BOOK

I have split the book into two parts. Part 1, Getting Started, contains the nuts and bolts. You don't need to read it all before you get started, but it's good to familiarise yourself.

Part 2 contains all of the spells and potions. Allow yourself to get familiar with the tools that you will need and the ritualistic set-ups (e.g. How to Build your Altar, on page 21), which will be helpful for most of the spells in this book.

**ALWAYS REMEMBER TWO OF THE MOST IMPORTANT THINGS
THAT YOU NEED WHEN CREATING SPELLS
ARE YOUR INTENTION AND YOUR INTUITION.**

Be focused on what you are about to invoke and be aware that the spell you are creating and the vibrations that you are sending out have the potential to totally change your life. You are sending out an energy signal to the universe and the act of creating a ritual is planting a seed in your subconscious mind, which in turn puts you in the correct vibrational frequency to receive what you are asking for.

After doing certain spells you may notice some special synchronicities. When this happens, take it as a sign from the universe that you are enough and that the universe has got your back and the magic is starting to work.

If something intuitively doesn't feel right or you have a question about the spell you are about to cast, refer to the pendulum (see page 34) for guidance.

If there is an ingredient in one of the spells that doesn't work for you, whether that is a scent that you don't like or don't have a connection with, or something you're allergic to, then don't use it! In this situation feel free to turn to the Glossary of Herbs (see page 150) and replace it with something that you feel more drawn to (top tip: rosemary works as a substitute for lots of herbs if you put your intention into it).

MOON PHASE ICONS

I have added a moon phase icon along with each spell, so you know which time of the month will be the most powerful for each spell and potion. Although it must be said, if you need to perform a banishing spell when there happens to be a new moon, don't let it stop you. Sometimes things can't wait and urgent spell work is required!

| NEW | WAXING | QUARTER | FULL | WANING |

PART 1

GETTING STARTED

BASIC
TOOLKIT

An outfit of empowerment

I always recommend getting dressed into something that feels empowering when you are about to make a spell and perform a ritual. In doing this you are marking the occasion and acknowledging that you are about to put your intention into something important. Getting a little dressed up can help you focus and be more aware and more conscious of the moment. You are performing a ritual that is about to have a massive positive impact on your life, so your fleece onesie won't cut it!

However, if you are performing magic on the move, I suggest that you close your eyes and visualise yourself putting on your imaginary cosmic sparkly cloak. (Don't forget to take it off when the spell is done!)

The right headspace

You want to be as calm and as 'in the zone' as possible before casting a spell, so having a little meditation beforehand will set the tone. A great breathing technique is to sit comfortably and close your eyes, then take some very gentle breaths in and out through your nose – count five in then seven or eight counts out. Repeat this about 10 or 15 times.

You can choose to have music on when you are mixing up your magic or do it in silence. Do whatever makes you feel good and focused.

Enchanting and blessing

This means charging a spell with your intention; it is a time to hold your hands over the ingredients of your potion or spell and bless them with your intent. Zone in on your power within, feel light and energy beaming through your fingertips blessing the spell, visualise the outcome, imagine how you will feel when your magic manifests into reality.

Mixing and blending

When you blend a spell or potion, remember that you should always stir clockwise to bring something into your life and anti-clockwise when you are banishing something.

I will talk a lot about mixing and blending in this book. Whenever this is mentioned, I mean blending with a mortar and pestle. Some ingredients are difficult to grind down completely, but try to get them to as fine a powder as possible.

Always remember, intent is the most powerful ingredient

It is important that you show the universe that you are willing and that you also have an action plan. If you are feeling a little stuck here, this can be a good time to draw a tarot or angel card or use a pendulum (see page 34).

Tools

---

mortar and pestle
glass jars
candles in various colours
crystals
(Note: please be sure if you are adding crystals to a tea,
tonic, oil or bath that they are polished stones and
not raw – the raw ones will tarnish in liquid.)
string in various colours
parchment or greaseproof paper
hot charcoal discs
tongs
ceramic/heatproof dish/cauldron/incense burner
salt or sand
compass

And...
good intentions

Most of the herbs that I mention in the book are ones that you may
find in your kitchen or are available in supermarkets or online.
I always use dried herbs in the spells, unless fresh are specified.
To cleanse dried herbs before you add them to your spells, crush
some cinnamon and burn it on a hot charcoal disc (see opposite
for full instructions), then pass the herbs through the smoke.
(This can also be done with copal resin or frankincense and myrrh.)

Once you have done this, you can store them with crystals. If you
are unsure which crystals to use, clear quartz is always a good idea.

HOT CHARCOAL GUIDE

Many of the incense blends in this book are to be burned on a hot charcoal disc, and you will need a small pair of tongs for heating these up. If you don't have any tongs, scissors or some tweezers will also do the job. Please don't do this with your hands as the charcoal gets very hot and you don't want to burn yourself (especially before a spell!). For extra insulation, add a generous layer of sand or salt to the heatproof dish you'll be using before you light the charcoal.

Using the tongs, hold the charcoal disc over a flame for 15–20 seconds, when the time is right the charcoal will start sparking. At this point, place the charcoal disc in a heatproof dish filled with salt or sand – this could be an incense burner, heatproof ceramic dish or cast-iron cauldron.

Always place a small pinch of your incense blend at a time onto the charcoal disc, being careful not to cover it entirely. You can keep adding the blend as you go on. The charcoal disc will usually burn for around 30 minutes. It will give off a lot of smoke, so make sure you are sitting away from a fire alarm.

ULTIMATE SPELL ACCESSORIES

These are a few items that are great to have in stock for giving spells superpowers.

Moon Water

Moon water is kind of like holy water to moon worshippers! While the moon is full, it is the perfect time to make the most of her shiny beaming rays and soak up her energy.

Water that has been charged up under a full moon can be used for anything that you think might need a little moon power. You can wash your crystals with it, add it to spells to give them an extra kick, drink it, add it to your bath water, or keep it on your altar.

YOU WILL NEED:
glass bottle or jug of water
(make sure it's filtered water if you plan to drink it)
crystals of your choice (optional)

1. Fill a glass bottle or jug with water and leave it outside under the moonlight to charge it up with the moon's superpowers. Add some crystals to the water for even more power.
2. Bring it inside before sunrise.

Black Salt

This is a multi-purpose salt that can be used to add superpower to banishing spells, and as a perfect accoutrement for protection and spells and to drive away evil.

YOU WILL NEED:

salt (sea salt is best, but any salt will do!)
charcoal from a hot charcoal disc or any burnt sage ash
spoon
bowl to blend and a jar to store it in

Blend the salt and charcoal in a bowl in an anti-clockwise direction, with a spoon, using your left hand. As you enchant the salt, say out loud, 'I banish you, go away, leave!'. Store it in a jar.

Moon Salt

Similar to Moon Water, this is a way to charge up salt with the full moon's potent rays and it will enhance the salt power in your spells. You can add it to your bath, to cleansing rituals, protection spells, or even use it when cooking.

YOU WILL NEED:

salt (sea salt is best, but any salt will do!)
1 clear quartz crystal
Bowl to blend and a jar to store it in

1. Leave a bowl of salt and a clear quartz crystal out beneath the moonlight for supercharged protection salt.
2. Bring it in before sunrise and store it in a jar.

Mojo Bags

Mojo bags, also known as charm bags, originate from the African folk magic that is Hoodoo. The charm bag can contain herbs, crystals or any charms that are special to you. They can be used for luck, love, prosperity, protection and psychic awakenings. Many of the incense blends in this book can be used in a mojo bag. Refer to the Glossary of Herbs (see page 150) or the Crystal Family Tree (see page 32) to make your own blends.

YOU WILL NEED:
*1 felt pouch in the colour corresponding
to your spell (see page 31)*

If you don't have a ready-made pouch you can make your own.

YOU WILL NEED:
*2 pieces of fabric 7 cm x 7 cm (2¾ in x 2¾ in)
needle, thread (the same colour as your pouch)
cord or string about 20 cm (8 in) long*

Sew the pieces of fabric together on one side. Flatten out the fabric and lay the piece of cord along the long side. Turn over the fabric to cover and secure the cord, then sew along the length to hold the cord in place. Fold in half down the middle seam, then stitch down one side, along the bottom and then up the other side, just up to the cord so that you can pull the cord to close the bag. Turn the bag right side out, then add the items to the bag. As you add your chosen items, talk to them and tell them what they each signify and what they are going to bring to you.

Note: always add a strand of your hair to the bag so that it is connected with you.

Before you seal the bag, take a moment to focus and visualise what you want it to do for you, and as you do this, blow what you are visualising and your intention into the bag, then pull the string tightly around the neck. Twist it around the top three times towards you and tie it in a knot so it is secure. It's always good to keep the bag on you, so fasten it with a safety pin to the inside of your waistband, so that it is touching your skin.

What to put in your mojo bag: herbs, crystals, charms, lodestones, magnets, a bay leaf, a piece of paper or a bay leaf with a sigil (see page 26) or words relating to what you would like your mojo bag to bring you. Also black cat hair for good luck and coins.

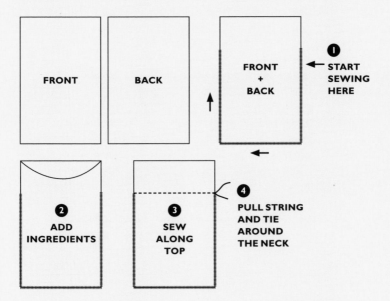

HOW TO DISPEL SPELL REMNANTS

If you have made a spell which is inviting or attracting something into your life, bury the remnants (ashes from a paper you've burned, for instance) in your front garden or leave it in a jar by your front door.

If it is for a brand new opportunity or a road opener, dispose of it on a crossroads that leads in four directions. This can be a little tricky to do, so if you don't have an appropriate junction nearby, you can also dispose of it by burying it near an evergreen tree.

If it is for something that you would like to keep, bury it in your back garden or in a plant pot outside.

If it is something that you would like to banish, bury it somewhere far away from your house, or if it is ashes from paper in a banishing spell, flush it down the toilet.

HOW TO
BUILD YOUR ALTAR

An altar is your sacred space, a special area where you can sit and meditate, manifest and mix up your potions and spells. You can really go to town as little or as much as you like with this area – it may be somewhere permanently dedicated to being your altar, or it may be a temporary set-up on your kitchen table, where you light a candle. It is entirely up to you.

Ideas for items to put on your altar: crystals, candles, any lucky charms you have collected along the way, incense, coins, flowers or some kind of offering (sweets, cake or nuts), angel cards, pictures of anyone special to you or pictures of any gods, goddesses, angels or deities that you feel a special empowering connection with.

The one rule I would suggest here is to keep your altar away from any electrical items. When you are sitting at it, try to have your phone switched off... I know there is always the temptation to post to Instagram and record the event, so if connecting to social media and sharing your ritual with friends is something that is important to you, that's fine. Just try to take a photo at the beginning of your session, then switch your phone off so you won't be disturbed and can be fully present in the moment.

You may also like to represent the elements at your altar. There are four elements, plus the spirit element, which represent the five points of the pentagram:

NORTH = EARTH	For this you can use a bowl of salt, sand or earth from a special place (maybe from beneath one of your favourite trees).
EAST = AIR	Here you can use a feather or smoke from some incense.
WEST = WATER	Here you can use some water with some clear quartz crystals in it or, even better, Moon Water (see page 16).
SOUTH = FIRE	In this direction you can have a candle of choice lit.
THE FIFTH POINT	Represents the spirit or the unseen, which is above and below and all around us.

You can also use crystals, to represent the elements. Here are a few of my favourites:

EARTH	Black tourmaline / Obsidian / Peridot
FIRE	Amber / Carnelian / Red Jasper
WATER	Amethyst / Moonstone / Celestite / Chrysocolla
AIR	Tiger's eye / Topaz / Lapis lazuli

HOW TO CAST A CIRCLE

A circle is a protected and sacred space in which you can create your spells. It is a magically charged space to separate and protect your magic work from what is going on in your everyday life that may interfere with the magic you are about to make.

I always find it quite reassuring that once I am in my magic circle, I instantly feel like I am in a high-vibing, positive mood and kind of like I'm in another world. You may even notice tingles or that there is a slight change in temperature.

Again, you can go all out or keep this simple, whatever you feel comfortable with and makes you feel empowered. Always remember that this is a totally safe place.

Here are three steps to cast your circle, you can choose to just do step one, or two or do all three, or create your own version.

STEP 1   Always start by cleansing the space with some sage or palo santo, you can then choose to either visualise surrounding yourself with a bubble of protective light. Or...

STEP 2   If you have some Moon Water and Moon Salt (see pages 16 and 17) you can blend them together and splash water around you in a clockwise direction, usually starting facing the east. And, if you wish:

STEP 3 Hold your hands out or point a crystal (clear quartz or amethyst is perfect here) in the direction in which you wish to start and turning to face each corner and call upon the spirits in each direction by saying:

EAST	*'Spirits of air, I call upon you to protect me within this circle.'*
SOUTH	*'Spirits of fire, I call upon you to protect me within this circle.'*
WEST	*'Spirits of water, I call upon you to protect me within this circle.'*
NORTH	*'Spirits of earth, I call upon you to protect me within this circle.'*

Carry on around the circle in a clockwise direction and as you face each direction repeat this action and say these words.

When you have finished, don't forget to close the circle. Do this by turning anti-clockwise and thanking the spirits in each of the directions for their presence. You may also choose to ring a bell, a singing bowl or even shake a box of matches in each direction when acknowledging these points of the circle.

Sometimes you may not have enough room to cast a circle; this is fine as there are many other options – you may want to light a candle in each direction, visualise yourself within a glowing circle of protective light, and imagine your guides and your spirit animals sitting beside you.

SIGILS

A sigil is a powerful symbol that you can create to represent your intention. This image can then be carved into a candle or drawn onto a piece of paper or a bay leaf with the relevant-coloured ink (see page 31). The idea is to create a symbol that you can remember so that it gets imbedded in your subconscious.

To start, you will need to write out your statement of intent. Use a nice pen and burn some Astral Travel Incense Blend (see page 64) or brew some Psychic Tea (see page 63) to assist your visions and creativity. When writing your statement of intent, always keep it positive and write it like you have already achieved it: I am happy, rather than I will be happy. So:

I AM HAPPY

Then cross out the vowels and any repeating letters:

MHPY

Start by practising on paper and take your time joining the letters up and moving them around – you can put them upside down or back to front if you want. You can really let your imagination run wild! As you draw, a doodle that you regularly do might come to mind, or you may feel some energy guiding you to add some spirals or dots. Imagine that you are looking at your designs through your Third Eye (see page 63), feel the energy and recognise a chill or a warm fuzzy feeling that you may feel as you are drawing. Make a symbol that you are proud of and that you have a connection with so that you can memorise what it looks like. Create a final draft when you're ready.

Once you have your symbol, to charge it up, hold it in your hands or put it beneath a crystal, then memorise what the symbol looks like. You can also charge your sigil under the full moon. Always make sure you have anointed your sigil with a bodily fluid for superpower (menstrual blood, saliva or sexual fluids) prior to burning.

You may choose to bless your sigil with an appropriate oil and then burn it; add it to a Mojo Bag (see page 18) with your favourite crystals; or crush it up to add superpower to an incense blend.

Note: These symbols contain a lot of power, so you may feel like you have drank a very large cup of coffee after a sigil-making session.

Here are some examples of sigils I have made up for inspiration, but I highly recommend taking some time to create your own so that you have something that you have a connection with.

I AM BALANCED
(MBLNCD)

I HAVE GOOD LUCK (HVGDLCK)

I AM PROTECTED (MPRTCD)

I AM SUCCESSFUL IN ALL MY ENDEAVOURS
(MSCFLNYDVR)

PSI BALLS
(MAGIC ON
THE MOVE)

A psi ball is a buildup of cosmic
energy that you can create
at your fingertips (literally).

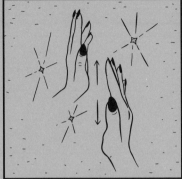

1 To begin, sit quietly with both feet firmly on the ground, then take a few nice, gentle deep breaths.

2 Next, place your hands together in a praying position and start to rub them together at a steady pace – not too fast or too slow – for 15–20 seconds.

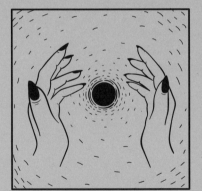

3 Then start to move your hands apart, slowly, just a little at a time. You should be able to feel the energy between your hands, so start to shape the energy into a ball. Play around with it until it feels like it's the right size. Focus on what your intention is (this can also be a healing energy that you want to send out to someone else or to yourself).

4 Blow your intention into the ball and release it out into the universe.

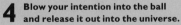

MAGICAL CORRESPONDENCES

Days of the week are connected to energetic vibrations of how the planets are aligned; this can help you decide which day might be more powerful for performing a spell or ritual.

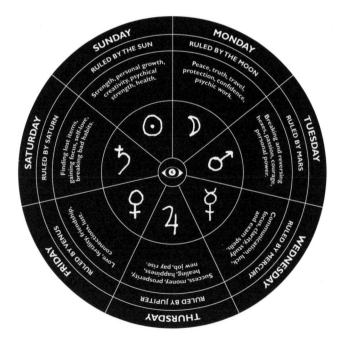

SUNDAY
RULED BY THE SUN
Strength, personal growth, creativity, psychical strength, health.

MONDAY
RULED BY THE MOON
Peace, truth, travel, protection, confidence, psychic work.

TUESDAY
RULED BY MARS
Breaking and reversing hexes, passion, courage, personal power.

WEDNESDAY
RULED BY MERCURY
Communication, luck, focus, clarity, study and exam spells.

THURSDAY
RULED BY JUPITER
Success, money, prosperity, healing, happiness, new job, pay rise.

FRIDAY
RULED BY VENUS
Love, fertility, friendship, connections, lust.

SATURDAY
RULED BY SATURN
Finding lost items, gaining focus, self-love, breaking bad habits.

Colours carry strong vibrational frequencies that can help connect you to your intentions. Their symbolic meanings are used in candles, mojo bags, inks and crystals – even in nail varnish and lipstick. Colour is also a great tool for using magic on the move, when you don't have time to make a spell. You can close your eyes and visualise the relevant colour surrounding your aura to assist in protecting you or drawing in what you want. These meanings are a guide; if you have your own personal connections with colours and what they mean, I suggest you explore those!

BLACK	banishing, breaking hexes, grounding.
BLUE	calming, healing, meditation, peace, forgiveness, inspiration.
GREEN	success, prosperity, freedom, abundance, money, good luck.
ORANGE	ambition, courage, luck, enthusiasm.
PINK	romance, affection, friendship, optimism, devotion, emotional healing.
PURPLE	psychic work, intuition spells, spiritual connection, wisdom.
RED	love, passion, power, attraction, fast action, willpower, courage.
WHITE	cleansing, truth, protection, new beginnings.
YELLOW	creativity, learning, communication, opening the door, concentration.

CRYSTAL FAMILY TREE

I like to think all my crystals have a bit of a character. To connect with them you can give yours a name and a little personality. Here is a family tree starring most of the crystals used in this book, to help you memorise what they can assist you with.

UNCLE
Labradorite

He loves all things metaphysical, he is a gifted psychic and has spent most of his life developing his intuition – he loves giving everyone tarot card readings. He recently went to his first plant medicine retreat and connected with his tribe from a past life.

AUNTIE
Amethyst

Amethyst is one hell of a charismatic lady. She is a healer and an empath, a bit of a hippy and full of energy. She works with people who have had childhood trauma and addictive personalities. She wears a lot of purple and is a huge Joni Mitchell fan.

MUM
Rose quartz

Rose quartz is universal, unconditional pure **LOVE**. She has everyone's back, is a great listener and gives **THE** best hugs!

COUSINS
Tourmaline   *Aventurine*

A bit of a bad boy that everyone loves. His brooding good looks mean that everyone has a crush on him! He's always in his leather jacket with hair greased back. He is a black belt in judo and loves the philosophies of martial arts. Strong and grounded, he is very protective over his family and friends.

Born lucky, he is always winning competitions, he enjoys a flutter on the horses and wins every time. He is a little bit of a wheeler dealer/entrepreneur and has the confidence to take a risk and go for it.

DAUGHTER
Smokey quartz

Smokey quartz is the ultimate big sister – if you have been stalking your crush on Instagram and get a bit jealous, she is the one to calm you down. She is amazing at reassuring you when you are having an insecure moment and always has the best advice.

BEST FRIEND
Moldavite

Quite a character, very intense and commanding. He's a mystical traveller, he disappears for long periods at a time and then always shows up just as you could do with some of his wisdom. He is a straight-talking, tough love kind of guy, but can be quite fierce and intimidating as he doesn't shy away from the truth.

GRANNY
Chrysocolla

Chrysocolla is like one of those legendary teachers you had at school that you will always remember; she was always encouraging you, helping to build your character, was full of wisdom, really gentle and able to calm any situation.

GRANDPA
Lapis lazuli

Lapis lazuli is like the grandpa who helps out in the local library since he retired from working in law. He is the intellectual of the family, loves the History Channel and a bit of *Judge Judy*. He is always very honest and if anyone is feeling a little unsure about a decision they have to make, they go straight to him.

DAD
Tiger's eye

Tiger's eye is definitely the dad of the family. He works as a psychologist and is a very understanding and compassionate man. Always very helpful, he has the best practical advice when guiding you through positive changes in your life.

UNCLE
Citrine

Citrine works as a life coach for CEOs and start-ups. He is 'Mr Strategic', he helps people strengthen their mental ability and focus and to reach their goals.

AUNTIE
Red Jasper

Red Jasper is a high-energy lady. She is a yoga teacher, she is full of vitality and loves doing mindfulness meditations. She loves spreading positive vibes.

AND HER SISTER
Moonstone

Moonstone is the sister/daughter on her gap year, she loves to travel and volunteer at schools, teaching art along the way. She is highly creative and has a great imagination.

COUSIN
Jet

Jet is one of the quietest members of the family, a sensitive, peaceful soul who enjoys quiet time. She works as an acupuncturist, helping people with stressful jobs and getting their energy flowing.

PENDULUM

If you are feeling a little stuck or unsure if it is the right time to do a spell, use this pendulum board as a guide.

If you can't get access to a pendulum, you can use a necklace or a crystal attached to a chain, or thread a piece of string through a whole nutmeg.

Before you start: say to the pendulum out loud that you give it complete permission to guide you to the right answer. Then swing the pendulum over the board and allow it to speak to you.

Quick tip: if you aren't near a pendulum board and are having an indecisive moment, you can ask a pendulum a yes or no question. Just ask it to show you which direction yes is and which direction no is, then ask your question and see which way it swings.

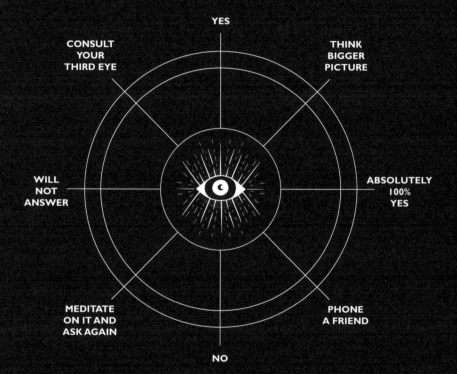

CASTING SPELLS
DURING CERTAIN
MOON PHASES WILL
GIVE THEM EXTRA
OOMPH!

MOONOLOGY

MOON CYCLES & SPELL WORK

Keeping track of the moon is easy to do, just download an app that will let you know what part of the cycle you're in and when to do particular rituals and spells.

New moon
The start of a cycle, this is the perfect time to plant seeds and set intentions, whether it's writing out your success action list for the coming cycle or it's manifestations for things you would like to call in and make happen. Write a letter with your intentions and thank the universe for the things you are manifesting as if you already have them. Ask for all sorts of things, big and small.

Waxing crescent to waxing gibbous
As the moon is growing, so should your manifestations. This is the time to nurture your ideas and a perfect time for prosperity spells. If you need motivation, draw an arrow going up on a bay leaf and anoint it with a few drops of lemongrass essential oil, then write a little manifesto of what you would like to see at this time. Use this time to take action, grow ideas, learn new things, develop your sense of self and embrace your determination.

Full moon
When the moon is full it's like the VOLUME IS TURNED UP! She is like a fully charged battery emitting extreme energetic moon rays. There is plenty of superpower to harness around this time. Yes, it is quite likely that at this time you may feel like an emotional wreck in LUNA-tic mode, but try not to worry, it happens to the best of us.

Try to embrace it, know that you are feeling like this because you are CONNECTED and you are tuned into her almighty frequencies. Put on your favourite song to dance to, play it loud, look up at her like she is a huge disco ball in the sky, hold your hands up and howl!

To make the most of this time, service your crystals, leave them out under the moonlight for cleansing and charging. Leave water, herbs and potions out and let the moon bless them with her magical power. If it's raining, collect the rainwater to use in spells, or blend it with some sandalwood essential oil and anoint yourself with it when you need some mystical full moon vibes.

Connect with the moon by taking a bowl of water and catching her reflection in it, then when the time feels right, place your hands in the bowl and let them soak up the moon water energy. When you feel like your hands are charged up, hold them up at the moon and soak up her energy while allowing your hands to dry naturally.

Alternatively, if you are feeling mega drained around this time, take a moment to relax and reflect on this past cycle and know that is it completed. It is the perfect time to think about what you have gratitude for, what has made you smile and laugh, who has warmed your heart and what you love about yourself.

Waning moon

This is when the moon appears smaller in size. This is the time to have a clear out, are there any situations that are taking up too much headspace, can you minimize any negative thinking patterns in your life? Check in with what isn't working for you and isn't serving you.

Dark moon

This is the night before a new moon, and it is the perfect time for making banishing spells and tying up loose ends. Clean your house for the new cycle, take a cleansing bath, do a purification spell.

FULL MOON &
ASTROLOGICAL SPELLS

Feel free to choose whichever spells feel right on the night, or
for a little guidance, work with astrological alignment. When an
astrological sign features in a full moon it can highlight which
areas and energies to focus on. This can be an effective time
to amplify spell work.

**FULL MOON
IN CAPRICORN**

Capricorn brings ambition and highlights which
goals need to be set. Tune in and be honest about
which tools you need to manifest to make things
happen and to move forward.

Write down what you want as if you already have it.
Or make a Sigil (see page 26) and charge it under
the moon alongside your crystals.

As this is the first full moon of the year, take a
ritualistic cleansing bath with a cup of Himalayan
salt, the juice of a lemon and clear quartz crystals.

For a spell, burn sandalwood chips and patchouli
essential oil. Hold your sigil or written
manifestations through the smoke. Sandalwood
will bless your intentions and send them into the
universe, and patchouli works a good vibes magnet.

**FULL MOON
IN AQUARIUS**

This is a time to allow the full moon to shine her spotlight right on you! Make time to reflect on what is working for you and what's not. Notice habits that are holding you back and work with shifting energy patterns that are no longer serving you; make space for new rituals that will help you gain focus, clarity and happiness in your life.

Blend one star anise and a pinch of mugwort using a mortar and pestle and place the ground mixture in a bowl with a smokey quartz crystal. Leave this out under the moonlight until sunrise then sprinkle the charged mixture under your pillow and keep the crystal with you until the next full moon. The crystal can be used for guidance until the next full moon (it's definitely worth keeping a little journal to see what comes up here).

**FULL MOON
IN PISCES**

Pisces moon is a time when psychic energies are high-vibing. So this is definitely a time to work with opening your third eye and take note of what you can see. Make a blend of third-eye-opening tea, and brew it to drink before bedtime (makes one pot).

YOU WILL NEED:
*2 teaspoons mugwort (do not drink if you
are pregnant)
½ cinnamon stick
pinch of dried rose petals
1 teaspoon dried marjoram*

**FULL MOON
IN PISCES
(CONTINUED)**

1. Blend all of the ingredients together with the intention of the tea being able to bring you a sign in your dream.
2. Add the ingredients to a teapot and add boiling water, then allow it to steep for at least 10 minutes before drinking.
3. As an alternative, you may choose to place a pinch of mugwort and a labradorite crystal under your pillow. Or for superpower you may wish to do both!

**FULL MOON
IN ARIES**

Aries moon is here to energise you and give you a boost for a new beginning. Embrace this energy with a power-project incense blend.

YOU WILL NEED:
pinch of dried rose petals
pinch of orris root powder
½ whole nutmeg
9 drops of benzoin essential oil
mortar and pestle
1 hot charcoal disc
heatproof dish
pen and paper

1. Blend all of the ingredients using a mortar and pestle.
2. Light a charcoal disc in a heatproof dish (see full instructions on page 15) and put a pinch of the incense onto the charcoal.
3. Write down your intention for your new venture and read it out loud to the smoke.

FULL MOON IN TAURUS

Taurus focuses on looking after money and checking that you are securing yourself financially. Use the water to water a plant (even better if it is a basil plant).

YOU WILL NEED:
money and security Sigil (see page 26)
glass bottle or container that holds
at least 250 ml (9 fl oz/1 cup)
1 citrine crystal
2 aventurine crystals

1. Write out a money and security sigil then tape the sigil to a glass bottle filled with citrine and aventurine. Add water to the bottle to cover crystals.
2. Leave the bottle outside under the full moon overnight to charge it up.
3. Bring it back inside before sunrise.

FULL MOON IN GEMINI

Gemini moon is all about communication and connections. To call in new friends, dress an orange candle in an upward motion with Attraction Oil (see page 104). Surround the candle with rosemary and salt.

This is also the perfect time to celebrate your friendships, create a gratitude group ritual. Drink mugwort tea and blend an incense together:

**FULL MOON
IN GEMINI
(CONTINUED)**

YOU WILL NEED:
*pinch of dried rose petals
pinch of dried lavender
½ pinch of frankincense resin
½ pinch of myrrh resin
mortar and pestle
2–3 hot charcoal discs (based on how
many friends are participating)
heatproof dish*

1. Blend all the ingredients using a mortar and pestle – take turns blending in a clockwise direction and passing the mortar around in a clockwise circle.
2. Light a few charcoal discs in a heatproof dish (see full instructions on page 15) and take turns adding a pinch of the incense while you hold hands and express gratitude for the group.

**FULL MOON
IN CANCER**

Time to practise self-love and celebrate what you love about yourself and what makes you happy.

YOU WILL NEED:
*300 g (1 cup) Himalayan salt
5 drops of lavender essential oil
5 drops of orange essential oil*

1. Take a bath with the salt and add the lavender and orange essential oils. Or prepare yourself a tea (makes one pot).

YOU WILL NEED:
1 batch of Moon Water (see page 16)
1 fresh rosemary sprig
pinch of fennel seeds
1 tablespoon loose chamomile tea

1. As you add all the ingredients to a teapot, visualise all of the things you love about yourself.
2. Add the ingredients to a teapot and add boiling water, then allow it to steep for at least 10 minutes before drinking.

You can also make this tonic:

YOU WILL NEED:
1 fresh rosemary sprig
pinch of fennel seeds
1 rose quartz crystal
glass bottle or jug that holds at least
250 ml (9 fl oz/1 cup)

1. Add the herbs and a rose quartz crystal to a glass bottle or jug of filtered water. Charge under a full moon and bring the mixture inside before sunrise.
2. Strain the herbs, then add the water back to the bottle with the rose quartz.
3. You can choose to drink this water in one go or store it and sip a little at a time, or add it to tea or drink it when self-love and reassurance is needed.

**FULL MOON
IN LEO**

Leo is here to support you with tapping into and unlocking your personal power. This is a perfect time to blend some Power Oil (see page 75).

Make a personal power Sigil (see page 26) and anoint it with Power Oil (see page 75). Spend some time in the moonlight memorising your power sigil, let it sit deep within your subconscious so that you can tap into it any time. You can choose to burn it or soak up the moon's energy and keep it in your purse or pocket.

**FULL MOON
IN VIRGO**

Virgos tend to be (slightly!) neat freak-y, so this is the perfect time to make the most of this Virgo energy – get organised and de-clutter. A motivation tea will help (makes one pot).

YOU WILL NEED:
2 teaspoons gotu kola
1 lemongrass dried stalk
1 teaspoon dried mint
1 piece of fresh ginger

1. As you add all the ingredients to a teapot, visualise yourself having motivation to get stuff ticked off your list.
2. Add boiling water, allow it to steep for at least 10 minutes. As you drink the tea, close your eyes and imagine the feeling that you will feel when you have completed all of your tasks. Once the tea is finished, get to work!!!

**FULL MOON
IN VIRGO
(CONTINUED)**

If you feel the tea won't be enough, combine it with this action incense:

YOU WILL NEED:
pinch of yarrow
pinch of thyme
9 drops of lemongrass essential oil
hot charcoal disc
heatproof dish

1. Blend all the ingredients and add to a hot charcoal disc (see full instructions on page 15). As this incense burns, look into the smoke and experience the sense of satisfaction that everything is organised and de-cluttered.

**FULL MOON
IN LIBRA**

A Libra full moon is time to check out balance in your life. Are your female and male energies aligned?

YOU WILL NEED:
1 large yellow candle
11 drops of vetiver essential oil
11 drops of bergamot essential oil
piece of yellow string

1. Anoint the candle with vetiver and bergamot essential oils and tie a piece of yellow string around it. Burn the candle for seven days then tie the string around your wrist.

FULL MOON IN SCORPIO

The intensity of Scorpio is the perfect time to embrace your sexual energy and connect with passion.

YOU WILL NEED:
2 tablespoons fennel seeds
2 tablespoons damiana
small jug (pitcher) of red wine

1. Add the ingredients to a small jug and leave out under the full moon overnight to charge, then bring it back inside before the sunrise and drink it for a special occasion. Lasts one week.

FULL MOON IN SAGITTARIUS

Sagittarius moon is a time to embrace your free spirit and nurture being inquisitive and curious. This is a very good time to set an intention to travel.

YOU WILL NEED:
Sigil on a fresh bay leaf (see page 26)
8 drops of mint essential oil
candle
compass

1. Memorise the sigil so that it is stored within your subconscious. Anoint your sigil with the mint essential oil.
2. Locate the direction of where you want to travel on the compass and burn the sigil over the flame of a candle in that direction.

PART 2

SPELLS

&

POTIONS

MAGNET MANIFESTATION

YOU WILL NEED:
pen and paper
3 lodestones (if lodestones aren't
available use small disc magnets)

When working with lodestones you are using their magnetic power to summon what you want towards you.

Write down your manifestations and place the paper in between the magnets to attract your wishes. You can anoint it with Attraction Oil (see page 102) for some added oomph.

ESSENTIALS

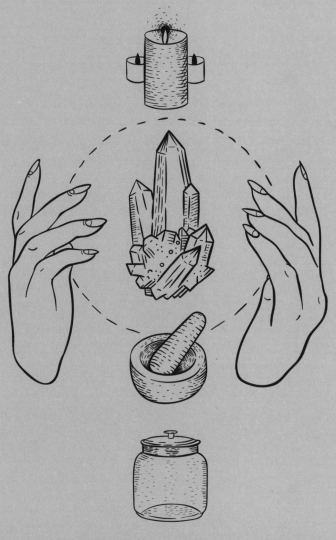

SPIRIT GUIDE MORNING BLESSING

YOU WILL NEED:
3 cm (1 in) stem dried lavender (or 1 pinch, if ground)
pinch of frankincense resin
7 drops of bergamot essential oil
bowl for blending
hot charcoal disc
heatproof dish

What better way to start the day than with an offering to all of your guides and spirit animals? Use this blessing to breathe love out to them and thank them for always having your back.

1. Blend the lavender, frankincense resin and bergamot essential oil in a small bowl in a clockwise direction, and as you do this focus on the unseen and the energies that are around you and support you every day.
2. Light a charcoal disc in a heatproof dish (see full instructions on page 15) and drop a small pinch of the offering on it at a time. As you do this, breathe in love from the energies that surround you and breathe out love out to them. Thank them for having your back and wish them and yourself an amazing day.

START
THIS SPELL
AFTER YOUR
MORNING
WASH AND
DRESS FOR THE
OCCASION!

MAGIC CLEANSING SPELL

YOU WILL NEED:
pinch of dried rosemary
pinch of dried sage
mortar and pestle
bowl for blending
3 drops of frankincense essential oil
hot charcoal disc
heatproof dish

**This spell works like a spiritual shower for your hands and any
of the tools or crystals that you are using in your spells – kind of
like a magical way of washing the dishes! It clears negativity and
banishes bad vibes, and also works as an offering to bless and
protect yourself and your magical apparatus.**

1. Blend the rosemary and sage using a mortar and pestle. When
    it is blended, place the mixture in a separate bowl and add the
    frankincense essential oil.
2. Blend the oil and herbs with your finger and as you do this,
    visualise an energy of white light cleansing and purifying, then
    place your hands over the spell, close your eyes and enchant
    them, blessing them with your intention of purification.

3. Light a charcoal disc in a heatproof dish (see full instructions on page 15). Add the oil to the charcoal. As the smoke rises, hold your hands and any of the tools that you wish to cleanse over the smoke to cleanse yourself before or after making potions.

SPELL TO OVERCOME ANXIETY

YOU WILL NEED:
pen and piece of yellow or white paper
pinch of dried yarrow
pinch of dried thyme
candle

This is a quickie spell to pass your worries on to the herbs who will send love and healing to whatever you are feeling anxious about.

1. Write down your worries on a piece of yellow or white paper, sprinkle some yarrow and thyme in the middle and visualise these powerful herbs dissolving your anxieties.
2. Fold the paper over three times and burn it over a candle in the direction of where the sun sets.

ANTI-ANXIETY TEA

MAKES ONE POT
YOU WILL NEED:
2 tablespoons dried valerian root
3 tablespoons loose chamomile tea
2 tablespoons dried lemon balm
5 rose quartz crystals (to store with the blend
and hold on to for extra comfort)

This tea is best drunk in bed at nighttime – ideally after a bath with five rose quartz crystals.

1. Add the ingredients to a teapot and add boiling water, then allow it to steep for at least 10 minutes before drinking. As you sip slowly on the tea, close your eyes and know that this feeling will pass. Close your eyes and breathe slowly and as you sip slowly on the tea, try to think back and remember a time when you weren't feeling like this. Feel your guides around you giving you a big hug – they are radiating you with energy to help this feeling pass.
2. Use the rose quartz crystals to store in a jar and activate the herbs.

SPELL TO BRING ABOUT CHANGE

This spell is perfect if you are feeling a little stuck, or if a situation in your life is moving slowly and needs a little kick up the bum.

1. Write down something that you would like to change in your life.
2. Find an oak tree.
3. Sit beneath the tree and visualise what it is that you want to change.
4. Bury what you have written down beneath the tree.
5. Leave the tree an offering, like a crystal or a piece of cake.
6. Take a leaf from the tree (make sure you ask permission first) and carry it around with you (or leave it on your altar beneath a tiger's eye crystal).

PSYCHIC
AWARENESS

○

If your third eye is feeling a little
blurry, rub a sprig of fresh rosemary
on your temples for a bit of psychic
guidance. (If you pick it yourself,
please remember to ask the plant's
permission first.)

THIRD EYE

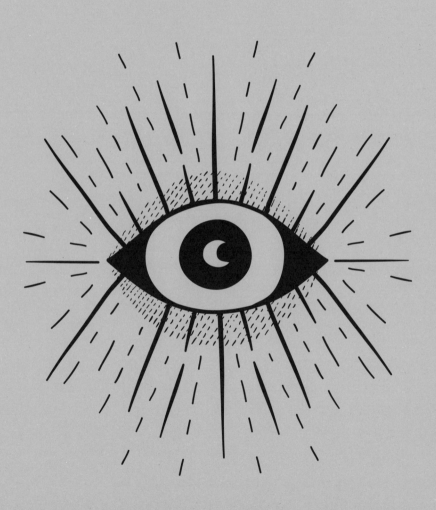

QUICK
INTUITION QUESTION

YOU WILL NEED:
3 drops of frankincense essential oil
1 fresh bay leaf
mortar and pestle
hot charcoal disc
heatproof dish
pen and notebook

This spell is perfect if you need to check in with your intuition. Always remember you are probably asking a question for a reason, and your first feeling about the situation is probably the right one.

1. Drop the frankincense oil on the bay leaf. As you rub in the frankincense, think of your question or, even better, ask it out loud.
2. Blend the bay leaf using a mortar and pestle, stirring in a clockwise direction. Light a charcoal disc in a heatproof dish (see full instructions on page 15) and place the bay leaf over the charcoal.
3. Breathe in the smoke and use your third eye to visualise the answer to your question. Have a pen and notebook handy and write down whatever messages you receive.

PSYCHIC
TEA

●◖◐○◗

MAKES ONE POT
YOU WILL NEED:

1 teaspoon dried rose petals
½ teaspoon loose jasmine tea
pinch of dried thyme
1 heaped tablespoon mugwort (do not drink if you are pregnant)
½ pinch of saffron threads (not totally needed,
but add for suuuuuuperpower)
pen and notebook

This is a tea to drink at bedtime, and then go to sleep with a pen and notebook next to your bed. It works best if you have a specific question, which might be something like, 'Where will I meet my future partner?', 'Should I change my job?', 'What areas of my life do I need to take better care of?'

When you wake up in the morning (or in the middle of the night) close your eyes, try to disconnect from your conscious brain and write down your thoughts, however weird. If the tea works instantly, write down what comes to mind immediately.

Add the ingredients to a teapot and add boiling water, then allow it to steep for at least 10 minutes before drinking.

ASTRAL TRAVEL INCENSE BLEND

YOU WILL NEED:
pinch of ground cinnamon
pinch of frankincense resin
mortar and pestle
hot charcoal disc
heatproof dish

**You can burn this before bedtime and repeat the
instructions as with the Psychic Tea on page 63.
The blend can be used alone, but for mega psychic
awakenings, burn it while you are drinking the tea.**

Blend the ingredients in a mortar and pestle. Light a
charcoal disc in a heatproof dish (see full instructions
on page 15) and burn the blend on your bedside table.

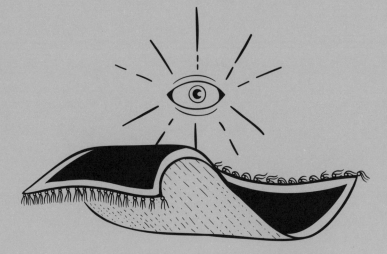

COURAGE
OIL

YOU WILL NEED:
1 smokey quartz crystal
pinch of dried thyme
pinch of dried yarrow
5 drops of geranium essential oil
20ml (½ fl oz) carrier oil of choice
glass jar or bottle
pinch each of dried orris root and rosemary (optional)
hot charcoal disc and heatproof dish (optional)

This is perfect before a job interview or speaking engagement. Anoint yourself or carry the jar with you.

1. Place all the ingredients in a jar or bottle and, before sealing it, blow your intention and visualisation in.
2. For superpower, and to add a little domination and control to this spell, light a charcoal disc in a heatproof dish (see full instructions on page 15) and burn a tiny pinch of orris root and a full pinch of rosemary over the charcoal. Pass your spell jar through the smoke nine times.

COURAGE

CONFIDENCE AND TRUST YOUR INNER VOICE OIL

YOU WILL NEED:

9 drops of thyme essential oil
pinch of dried yarrow
100 ml (3½ fl oz/½ cup) carrier oil (almond or jojoba)
1 chrysocolla crystal
glass jar or container

When you need a hit of courage at the ready, try this spell.

1. Place all the ingredients in a jar and leave it out in the moonlight overnight to charge up (doing this during a full moon would be best, but, this spell is meant to be speedy so don't worry if you have to make it the night before). Make sure to bring it inside before sunrise.
2. Wear the oil and carry the crystal in your pocket.

COURAGE TO WALK IN THE RIGHT DIRECTION

YOU WILL NEED:
1 heaped teaspoon coconut oil
5 drops of peppermint essential oil
bowl of warm water

If you are in two minds about something and have to make a decision later on in the day, use this spell in the morning to help you make a decision.

1. Place the coconut oil in a bowl of warm water and blend with the peppermint oil in a clockwise direction.
2. Use the warm mixture to massage your feet for confidence in walking in the right direction.

CRYSTAL OF COURAGE BLESSING

YOU WILL NEED:
1 teaspoon dried yarrow
½ teaspoon fennel seeds
generous pinch of dried rose petals
mortar and pestle
10 drops of thyme essential oil
100 ml (3½ fl oz/½ cup) almond oil
glass jar or bottle
citrine or smokey quartz crystal (or both!)

This oil is great for times you are feeling nervous about something, maybe a job interview, a difficult conversation or public speaking. Anoint yourself with it, add it to your bath, or write down what you need to find the courage for and anoint the paper. If it is a letter that you have to write, anoint the pen that you are writing the letter with.

1. Blend the herbs and rose petals using a mortar and pestle, and as you do so, visualise yourself taking action and finding the courage to take action.
2. Add the oils to a glass jar or bottle then add the blended herbs.

3. Whisper your intention to your crystal, put it in the jar or bottle and seal the lid.

4. Leave the mixture overnight and allow your crystal to charge up all of the superpowers of the herbs. When you are ready, remove the crystal from the jar and keep it close. This mixture can be saved and used again to charge up your crystals, or these oils and herbs can be added to a bath for some super power.

WARRIOR SPELL

YOU WILL NEED:
1 small citrine crystal
3 pinches of dried thyme
1 piece of fresh ginger (about the size of a thumbnail)
piece of red fabric
red thread
1 needle
strand of your hair

1. Place the citrine crystal, thyme and ginger on the piece of red fabric for superpower.
2. Call out to any protective warrior guides and energies to come and assist you with charging up and blessing your spell.
3. Place your hands on the blend and feel the energy of your guides assisting you with warrior-type powers of courage and strength.
4. Create a Mojo Bag (see page 18 for full instructions), sewing in a clockwise direction. When you are at your last seam that needs joining, blow in your intention of warrior energy and strength. Add a strand of your hair to the mojo bag to connect with it. Finish sewing up and keep it with you at all times.

Extra power: put a few drops of thyme essential oil onto the bag and inhale whenever you need a boost of your inner warrior.

THIS TONIC WILL PREPARE YOU WHEN YOU NEED

THE STRENGTH OF A WARRIOR

BRILLIANT
FOR ASKING
FOR
A PAY RISE
AT WORK

PERSONAL POWER OIL

YOU WILL NEED:
3 pinches of dried thyme
1 small piece of fresh ginger
9 drops of orange essential oil
100 ml (3½ fl oz/½ cup) almond oil
pinch of orris root
1 amethyst crystal
glass jar or bottle

This is the perfect blend to help you if you feel you have lost your voice or are having trouble speaking up (brilliant for asking for a pay rise at work), or assisting you when you are refusing to do something you don't want to, or helping you get out of bed on a day when you can't summon up any energy.

You can also anoint crystals and any manifestations or sigils with this. So make a jar of this as it always comes in handy, and like fine wine, it gets better with age!

1. Place all the ingredients in a jar or bottle and blow your intention in before you seal it.
2. You can place this under a full moon any time for an energy top-up.

SELF-LOVE AND EMPOWERMENT SPELL

YOU WILL NEED:
2 pinches of dried rose petals
pinch each of dried thyme, yarrow and rosemary
5 whole cloves
pinch of ground cinnamon
pinch each of frankincense and myrrh resin
mortar and pestle
hot charcoal disc
heatproof dish

This is a spell to banish the negative voice inside your head, the voice that makes you compare yourself to others, speaks to you negatively and makes you feel like you aren't good enough.

This is also a great general spell to do before any manifesting or intention setting, because when you are manifesting from a place of self-love you will know exactly the right things to call in. If there is any of this left over, store it with a rose quartz crystal next to your bed. This is also a lovely spell to do with your friends.

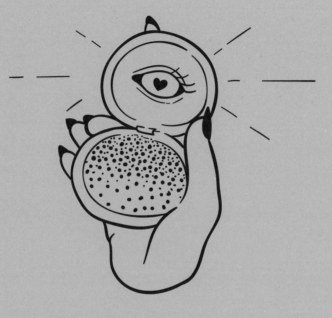

1. Blend all the herbs and resins, using a mortar and pestle, in a clockwise direction, thinking of love surrounding you. Feel your spirit guides close your eyes, pat your back, then whisper in your ear how wonderful you are, and how you are here because the universe needs you.
2. Light a hot charcoal disc in a heatproof dish (see page 15 for full instructions) and add a pinch of the herbs, saying, 'I am enough'.
3. For the following few days after performing this spell, look out for special signs from the universe.

DECISION MAKER

YOU WILL NEED:
1 blue candle
7 drops of rosemary essential oil

**This is an indecisiveness antidote.
Recognise the first feeling that you have
in your gut. If you are still unsure, refer
to the pendulum board on page 34.**

1. Anoint your candle with the rosemary
   essential oil in an upwards motion.
2. Light the candle and stare at its flame.
   Focus on whatever needs a decision and
   think of the possible outcomes, notice
   how the flame flickers for your answer.

CONSULT YOUR WISDOM TEA

MAKES ONE POT
YOU WILL NEED:
1 teaspoon dried sage
1 teaspoon dried mint
1 tiger's eye crystal

All of the answers are deep within you, so let this tea guide you to your deep wisdom.

If you have a specific question, write it down before you drink this tea. Take some long, slow, gentle deep breaths and sip the tea slowly, close your eyes and allow yourself to have a meaningful and loving conversation with your inner wisdom.

Allow the tea to hush your inner critic from the conversation, and connect in the knowledge that your inner wisdom will only ever speak to you from a place of love and encouragement.

1. Add the ingredients to a teapot and add boiling water, then allow it to steep for at least 10 minutes.
2. Drink the tea slowly while holding onto your tiger's eye crystal.

THE
BODYGUARD

YOU WILL NEED:

150 ml (5¾ fl oz/¾ cup) almond oil
9 drops of bergamot essential oil
9 drops of sage essential oil
glass jar or bottle
1 black tourmaline crystal

A bodyguard's job is to protect their clients from harm; they stand in the background – cool, calm and collected – and keep whoever they are looking after feeling safe and grounded. They stare down any negative vibes that come your way.

1. Add the oils to the jar or bottle, pop the lid on and shake it up, then add the crystal. Leave the mixture to charge overnight (preferably under a full moon).
2. Rub this oil on your hands for ultimate protection.

PROTECTION

HOODOO CASCARILLA PROTECTION SPELL

YOU WILL NEED:
6 washed-out empty eggshells
5 pinches of dried sage
3 pinches of Black Salt (see page 17) for
superpower (optional)
mortar and pestle
pen and paper

Cascarrilla powder is made from eggshells ground down to a fine sand. It originates from Hoodoo and Santeria traditions, which believe that the delicate eggshells hold strong protective powers that can protect a life within. This spell gives any purification spell some punch. For extra super power, sprinkle the salt in the shape of a circle around the picture or piece of paper, then light five white candles around the salt. Always remember to ask permission before doing a spell for anyone other than yourself.

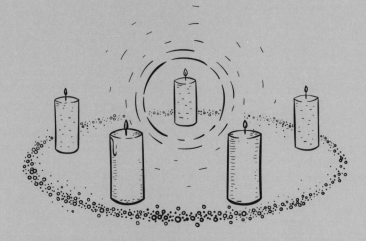

1. Blend all of the ingredients together into a fine powder using a mortar and pestle. Enchant and visualise a bright white protective light.
2. You can sprinkle the mixture around your house, on your doorstep for protection, or take or find a photo of someone who needs protection. Write their name on a piece of paper, or if it's a situation that needs protection rather than a person, write that down on a piece of paper.

PROTECTION POTION ON THE GO

YOU WILL NEED:
1 clear quartz crystal
pinch of dried rosemary

A little quickie that you can prepare then store in a bottle and carry around with you to sip on throughout the day, giving you protection on the go.

Add the crystal and rosemary to your drinking water for protection in a hurry.

HOLIDAY INSURANCE
AMULET

YOU WILL NEED:
7 juniper berries
1 dried bay leaf
3 cloves
pinch of dried sage
1 amethyst crystal
pinch of Black Salt (see page 17) for superpower (optional)

Pop this into your bag to keep yourself and your belongings protected on trips. A lovely gift idea for friends.

1. Blend all of the ingredients with the intention of safe travels and amazing adventures.
2. Place the herbs in an amulet or blue Mojo Bag (see page 18). (If this spell is for a friend, tell them to place a strand of their hair in it to connect them to it.)

TRAVEL SPELL

YOU WILL NEED:

a picture of the destination you wish you travel to
compass
1 batch of of Attraction Oil (see page 102)
1 lodestone (or a round magnet)

Holidays are an important necessity in life... Use this spell to assist with calling in your next trip away.
Use the compass to work out which direction the destination you wish to travel is.

1. Place the picture (or the name of the destination written on a piece of paper) in the direction of where you wish to travel.
2. Anoint your picture with the Attraction Oil.
3. Place a lodestone on the picture and leave it there.
4. You can keep adding attraction oil while you wait for the trip to happen.

HOT FOOT SPELL TO REMOVE UNWANTED VISITORS

YOU WILL NEED:
1 batch of Black Salt (see page 17)
2 pinches of cayenne pepper
the shoes of the person you want to leave!

Use this 'hot foot powder' when you would like someone to leave your property. Be warned, it's a fast-acting spell.

1. Blend the black salt and the cayenne pepper together in an anti-clockwise direction.
2. Place both shoes facing the door. Add a pinch of the blend in each shoe. Get ready to hand them their coat and say seeeee ya later!

ENERGY PROTECTION POTION FOR EMPATHS

YOU WILL NEED:
3 pinches of fennel seeds
5 drops of vetiver essential oil
100 ml (3½ fl oz/½ cup) carrier oil of your choice
glass jar or bottle
1 labradorite crystal

If you are an empath you probably tend to be tuned in to your intuition and can absorb energy and vibes from people around you. This may also leave you feeling a little drained and exhausted or even resentful to someone who has come to you for a chat. Here is a spell to cleanse and recharge your special empath soul and to be worn around energy vampires!

1. Blend the seeds and oils together in a glass jar or bottle, then add the crystal.
2. Keep the crystal in the jar or bottle and anoint yourself as a shield from soaking up unwanted energies and feeling emotionally drained.

VISUALISATION TIP:

IN EXTREME CASES,

VISUALISE YOURSELF

SURROUNDED BY A

MIRROR, REFLECTING

BACK ANY NEGATIVE

ENERGY OR ANY OF

THE ENERGY THAT

YOU DO NOT WISH

TO ABSORB

SPIRITUAL CLEANSING BATH

YOU WILL NEED:
*candles (white are good, but
any colour will work)
pinch of dried or fresh sage
10 drops of peppermint essential oil
150 g (½ cup) Himalayan salt or Epsom salts
(any salt will do if you can't get access to either of these)
1 clear quartz (but you could use 10 or 20!)
white clothing (optional)*

Sometimes negative energy can have a build-up and leave you feeling drained. Having a bath can be a spiritual form of cleansing your aura, washing away a bad day or some heavy energy you may feel that you have been carrying around.

Take a spiritual bath and know that when all the water has disappeared down the drain, it has taken away the negativity you were holding on to and it's time for a new beginning.

1. Light some candles and add the ingredients to your bath along with the quartz. Soak yourself and visualise white cleansing light. When you step out of the bath, be conscious that the water going down the drain is taking away negativity.
2. After your bath, wear white clothes (if you like) for the next eight hours as a reminder that you have reset yourself.

Extra power: If you are cleansing something specific, write it down on a piece of paper and burn it with a black candle before your bath.

REVERSE NEGATIVITY
SPELL AND HEX-BREAKING

YOU WILL NEED:
pinch of dried basil
pinch of dried rose petals
pinch of dried lavender
1 dried bay leaf
pinch of dried rosemary
10 drops of eucalyptus essential oil
bowl for mixing

Sometimes it might feel like you are experiencing a run of bad luck, or maybe you feel like someone is thinking negatively towards you. Or maybe you have broken a mirror and are feeling superstitious. This spell will bless you with love and protection and put a stop to any negativity. When the negativity has been banished, it will leave an energetic space... Think about what energy you would like to fill this space with and invite it in.

1. Blend all the ingredients in a bowl.
2. Run a bath and add the herbs. Bathe for at least 20 minutes.
3. Gather the mix from your bath and bury it somewhere far from your house. If you can't travel far, flush it down the toilet.

TO REMOVE NEGATIVITY FROM YOUR HOUSE

YOU WILL NEED:
skin from 1 garlic bulb
pinch of dried rosemary
pinch of dried sage
pinch of cumin
3 drops of eucalyptus essential oil
mortar and pestle

Blend the herbs using a mortar and pestle, in an anti-clockwise direction, and burn to remove any jinxes or curses.

MERCURY RETROGRADE SPELL

MAKES ONE POT
YOU WILL NEED:
1 valerian root
1 teaspoon wild lettuce extract
1 teaspoon dried lavender
1 vanilla bean, cut into small pieces
1 tourmaline crystal

When mercury is in retrograde it's always a funny old time. You may notice that things get lost in the post, electrical items break down and you might experience problems communicating. This is a good time to sit back, slow down and reassess everything that has been happening in your life. Reassess, reevaluate, review... and RELAX! Drink this grounding tea in the evening to help you process your day.

1. Add the ingredients, except the crystal, to a teapot and add boiling water, then allow it to steep for at least 10 minutes.
2. Drink the tea whilst holding on tight to your tourmaline. Keep the tourmaline close and drink the tea as often as you like until the mercury is out of retrograde and things go back to normal!

'CHILL,
IT'S MERCURY
RETROGRADE,'
SAID NO ONE
EVER!

SEND AWAY
ANGER SPELL

YOU WILL NEED:
vinegar (enough to fill half the jar)
1 lemon
handful of salt (any type will do,
so use your least favourite!)
glass jar or bottle
pen and paper
1 white candle

Send away anger and say see ya later to your RAGE, it is no longer serving you and holds no place in your life.

1. Blend the vinegar, the juice of the lemon (keep the lemon skin for later) and salt in the jar or bottle.
2. Write down whatever you are angry about. As you write I recommend you scream, shout, cry, hit a cushion and release your emotions and rage.
3. Fold the piece of paper three times in the direction away from you and place the paper in the jar.
4. Leave this in the jar for a minimum of three hours, then take the paper, roll it up and put it in the squeezed-out lemon halves.
5. Place the two halves of the lemon together and go somewhere far away and bury it. If you can't go anywhere too far, when it's dark then go and place it in a neighbour's bin or a public bin. As you dispose of it, know that this anger is no longer your problem.
6. Light the white candle and invite something positive into your life to replace the space that the anger you felt has left. Close your eyes and visualise yourself in your favourite place of nature and call in love and happiness.

STOP POTION!

YOU WILL NEED:
3 tablespoons salt
1 tablespoon cayenne pepper
120 ml (4 fl oz/½ cup) vinegar
juice of 1 lemon
3 juniper berries
glass jar or bottle
black marker pen
pen and paper

Use this spell as a spiritual stop button. Remember, you must close the door before a new one can open. If you want to do this spell for someone else, make sure that you ask for permission first.

1. Add everything to the jar except the juniper berries, then write down whatever it is that you want to stop on a piece of paper.
2. Write the word 'STOP' in a big black marker over the top.
3. Fold the piece of paper up as small as possible, each time folding it away from you. Put the paper in the jar.

4. Crush the juniper berries one at a time and each time you crush one, shout the word 'STOP', then drop them into the jar and know that this ingredient will dissolve whatever you wish to stop. When it feels right, usually three days later, remove the paper and bury it in the direction of the sunset.

LOVE
OIL

◯

YOU WILL NEED:
1 rose quartz crystal
handful of dried rose petals
2 cardamom pods
2 cinnamon sticks
10 drops of rose essential oil
pinch of dried sage
200 ml (7 fl oz/¾ cup) almond oil
glass jar or bottle

This is a multi-purpose oil that can be used for all types of love (not just romantic). Use this potion in your bath to call in love, anoint the corners of a love letter with it or rub it on your doorframe to invite love into your house. Be generous with this potion and share it with friends, spread magical loving vibes as you please.

Blend all of the ingredients together in a jar or bottle and leave outside overnight to charge under a full moon. Bring the mixture back inside before sunrise.

LOVE

ATTRACTION OIL

YOU WILL NEED:

20 ml (½ fl oz) almond oil
2 small cinnamon sticks
pinch of dried rose petals
9 whole cloves
9 drops of patchouli essential oil
9 drops of rose essential oil
1 lodestone
glass jar or bottle

This oil does what it says in the title... It works best if you have a specific person in mind – always be sure if you are thinking of someone when performing a love spell that this is the person you really want to call in.

The one rule I would always follow with a love spell is, if you are having to force it, maybe it's not meant to be – bear in mind that there might be someone soooooo much better on their way to you.

You can use this oil on a photo of someone you wish to attract, to anoint Sigils, your written manifestations, candles, crystals or add it to your bath or yourself on a night out!

Blend all of the ingredients together in a jar or bottle and leave outside overnight to charge under a full moon. Bring the mixture back inside before sunrise. This oil can be used to add super attracting power to any spell, but is especially powerful for love spells.

TO BRING
A LITTLE
SWEETNESS
AND LOVE
INTO
YOUR LIFE

LOVE
HONEY

YOU WILL NEED:

1 small piece of fresh ginger
1 jar of honey
1 rose quartz crystal
handful of dried or fresh rose petals
2 red candles

1. Cut the piece of ginger in half and place both pieces in the jar of honey along with the crystal.
2. Place rose petals in a circle around the jar and light the two candles on either side.
3. Allow both of the candles to burn down over two nights. Eat the honey or use it to sweeten your tea to call love into your life.

LOVE COME TO ME CANDLE SPELL

YOU WILL NEED:

pinch of dried or fresh rose petals
pinch of cardamom seeds
2 cinnamon sticks
pinch of dried or fresh rosemary
mortar and pestle
glass jar or bottle
9 drops of patchouli essential oil
150 ml (5 fl oz/½ cup) almond oil
(or carrier oil of your choice)
2 rose quartz crystals
2 pink candles

This is a love attraction oil, which will attract all sorts of love. During the three nights that you are burning this candle, make sure that when you leave the house you are walking with your head held high and your eyes are wide open to receive the love that is making its way to you. For superpower, use Love Oil here (see page 100) to anoint the candles in an upwards motion.

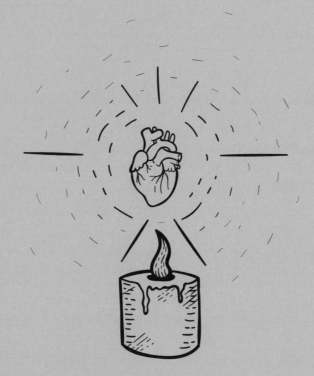

1. Blend all the herbs and spices together using a mortar and pestle and enchant with your desires.
2. Add the oil to a jar or bottle, then add your enchanted mixture and rose quartz crystals.
3. Light the pink candles on either side of your jar or bottle and burn for three nights.
4. Use the oil to anoint your body when you are in need of love.

THIS IS A LITTLE

SPELL TO DRAW

A LOVER

TO YOU THAT

YOU HAVE NOT

MET YET

BRING ME
A LOVER

YOU WILL NEED:
1 bunch of fresh red roses
vase
1 rose quartz crystal
1 envelope

After doing this spell, look out for random connections. Get yourself out there – go to a party, or out dancing, see if you lock eyes with anyone when on public transport or while walking round a park. Now might be the time to join a dating app.

1. Hold the bunch of red roses to your heart and send out love to the universe. Focus on breathing in love and send love out as you exhale.
2. Add the flowers to a vase filled with water and drop in the rose quartz to charge your roses with universal love.
3. Place the vase next to your bed so it's the first thing you see every morning and the last thing you see before you go to sleep. Make sure to smell the flowers every day.
4. On the fifth day, take off the rose petals, put them in an envelope and keep it close to your pillow. Know that love is on its way to you.

RED HOT SEX SPELL

YOU WILL NEED:
pen and paper
pinch of chilli powder
1 red candle

This will turn your lover into a freak between the sheets...

Write your lover's name on a piece of paper and sprinkle chilli powder over it. Light a red candle beside it and watch out!

FOR QUICK(IE) SUPERPOWER

YOU WILL NEED:
1 smokey quartz crystal
1 red carnelian crystal

For when you or your partner need a little help loosening up your inhibitions...

Place both crystals under your pillows before bedtime and go wild!

SPELL TO MAKE YOUR LOVER CALL YOU

YOU WILL NEED:
pen and a square piece of parchment or greaseproof paper
1 batch of of Attraction Oil (see page 102)

This spell is a STRONG one. If your lover doesn't call you within seven days, take it as a sign that the universe has your back and that a call from this person wouldn't work in your favour.

1. Write on a piece of paper the person you want to call you, nine times. As you write, visualise them calling you, then write your name on the paper.
2. Anoint the paper with Attraction oil on each corner (working in a clockwise direction). Each time you anoint a corner, say 'call me'.
3. Fold the paper three times towards you.
4. Place the paper under your phone and wait for the call!

QUICK VERSION

SAVE THE PERSON YOU'D LIKE
TO CALL YOU IN YOUR PHONE
UNDER THEIR FIRST NAME AND
'CALL ME' AS THEIR LAST NAME.
ANOINT YOUR PHONE WITH
ATTRACTION OIL AND VISUALISE
THE PERSON CALLING
OR MESSAGING YOU

HEARTBREAK CURE

YOU WILL NEED:
5 black peppercorns
pinch of cumin seeds
mortar and pestle
tears (optional)
5 drops of rose essential oil
hot charcoal disc
heatproof dish

Heartbreak is the worst, it can feel like the end of the world. Breathe in the healing aroma from this spell and know that it is sending messages of love and get well soon vibrations direct to your heart.

1. Blend the black peppercorns and cumin seeds into a powder using a mortar and pestle.
2. Add to the mix collected tear drops (optional) that have been cried over whoever has caused the heartache (you can also use the tears on your fingers while mixing up the paste). Add rose essential oil with the tears and mix into a paste.

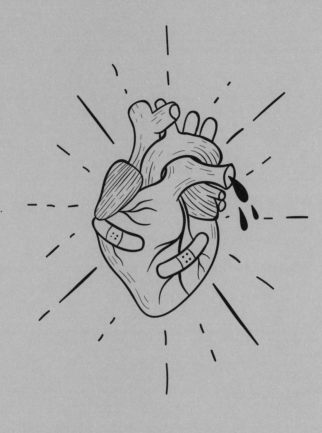

3. Light a charcoal disc in a heatproof dish (see full instructions on page 15) and put pinches of the potion on the charcoal.
4. Sit and watch the smoke. Cry as the smoke drifts and know that as you breathe it in your heart will be receiving healing loving energy and that soon you will be feeling better.

BANISH
AN EX

YOU WILL NEED:
image of the person you wish to forget,
or their name on a piece of paper
1 small piece of black cloth
3 pinches of Black Salt (see page 17)
needle and thread

This spell will cut the emotional cords when you no longer want a person to occupy your mind.

1. Place the piece of paper with the name or picture of the person you wish to forget in the centre of the black cloth and add the Black Salt with your non dominant hand.
2. Stitch up the cloth, say goodbye and bury it far away from your house (not in your garden!).

BREAK AND CUT BATH

YOU WILL NEED:
9 pinches of dried sage
9 black peppercorns
300 g (1 cup) salt – Himalayan is best,
but you can also use sea salt or Epsom salts
peel and juice of 1 lemon
bowl for blending
clear quartz crystals

This is a renewal bath, to cleanse away bad memories, bad relationships and hexes.

1. Mix the sage, lemon peel and peppercorns in a bowl in an anti-clockwise direction.
2. Run a hot bath, then add all of the blended ingredients and the lemon juice. Know that when you step out of the bath you will be fully cleansed and the reset button will have been pressed.

Extra power: Before you get in the bath, write down what you are breaking away from on a piece of paper and fold it three times in a direction that is away from you. Burn it with a black candle.

AIN'T GOT TIME
FOR THAT
(QUICK BANISHING SPELL)

YOU WILL NEED:
pen and paper
1 black candle

This banishing spell can also be done before manifesting. Remember, every time you banish something you are creating some room to invite something positive in.

Write the person's name or the situation that no longer serves you on a piece of paper and burn it over a black candle.

- If you don't have access to a black candle, any coloured candle will be fine.
- If you need to do a super-quick banish and don't have access to a candle, write it down and rip it up and flush it down the toilet.
- Alternatively, write down an ex's name on a piece of paper and put it in an ice cube tray, cover with water and place in the freezer.

SPIRITUAL SPEED

YOU WILL NEED:
3 black peppercorns
pinch of frankincense resin
mortar and pestle
hot charcoal disc
heatproof dish

To make you go, go go!

1. Crush the ingredients together using a mortar and pestle.
2. Light a charcoal disc in a heatproof dish (see full instructions on page 15) and burn the blend on the charcoal disc to make you go at super speed. This spell works fast!

Note: careful with this on a full moon!

MONEY &

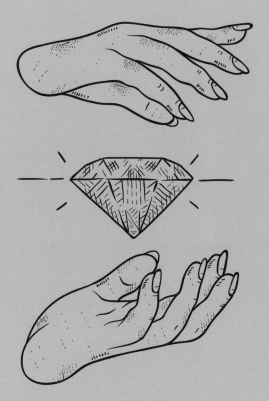

PROSPERITY

TOP TIP:

DON'T CALL
IT A TO-DO
LIST, CALL IT
A SUCCESS
ACTION LIST

MR MOTIVATOR

YOU WILL NEED:
pinch of dried thyme
pinch of dried rosemary
pinch of dried galangal
5 drops of lemongrass essential oil
mortar and pestle
hot charcoal disc
heatproof dish

This is the antidote to procrastination and will help you get everything ticked off your to-do list.

1. Blend the ingredients together using a mortar and pestle.
2. Light a charcoal disc in a heatproof dish (see full instructions on page 15) and burn the mixture.
3. As you burn, visualise the feeling that you will have once you have completed all of your tasks. As you visualise this, write out the list of everything that needs to be done.

BRING IN MORE BUSINESS

YOU WILL NEED:
1 cinnamon stick
1 teaspoon dried basil
5 whole cloves
1 whole nutmeg, grated
mortar and pestle

This spell will attract new clients and customers, which will bring money to your business.

1. Blend all of the ingredients using a mortar and pestle. Enchant and visualise money as an energy flowing freely into your life.
2. Sprinkle the mixture around your front door, then a little in your purse, visualising success as you do this.

TOP TIP:

KEEP A BOWL
OF CHANGE
BY THE FRONT
DOOR TO
KEEP MONEY
FLOWING
IN THROUGH
THE DOOR

ELEMENTAL MONEY SPELL

YOU WILL NEED:
5 whole cloves
10 drops of basil essential oil
mortar and pestle
1 green candle

A little financial boost brought to you with the assistance of the elements.

1. Grind the cloves using a mortar and pestle, in a clockwise direction, and blend with the basil essential oil. Enchant the herbs with a blessing of 'money is an energy, with it comes freedom and security'.
2. Keep repeating the chant as you anoint your candle with this blend in an upwards motion.
3. Place items representing all of the elements (see page 23) in the correct directions around the green candle and let it burn out over seven nights.

FAST MONEY SPELL

YOU WILL NEED:
1 piece of parchment paper or greaseproof paper
pen
1 batch of Attraction Oil (see page 100)
1 lodestone or 3 magnets (optional)

This isn't big money, it's fast money; you will find that small amounts of money come to you quickly. You may get booked for a freelance job, or you may find some cash in a pocket, old purse, or down the back of the sofa. You might make a quick sale on eBay, or perhaps someone who owes you money will pay you back.

1. Write on the parchment paper '£££ YOUR NAME £££'.
2. Anoint each corner of the paper with the Attraction oil in a clockwise direction, then fold the paper three times (each time folding towards you). As you do this, visualise and say out loud 'money, money come to me', three times.
3. Keep the piece of paper in your wallet or on your altar beneath a lodestone (or in between three magnets).

SPELL TO MAKE MONEY GROW

YOU WILL NEED:
3 pinches of dried patchouli
3 pinches of ground allspice
3 pinches of dried basil
mortar and pestle
1 gold- or silver-coloured coin
1 healthy plant (no dead leaves)

This spell is all about the long game; unlike a fast money spell, you may have to wait until the plant is in full bloom... Don't let this put you off, always remember that the best things come to those who wait!

1. Blend the patchouli, allspice and basil in a clockwise direction using a mortar and pestle while concentrating on your intent.
2. Bury the coin halfway down in soil of the plant pot then sprinkle the herbs around the soil.

MONEY ATTRACTION OIL

YOU WILL NEED:
9 whole cloves
3 pinches of dried peppermint
3 pinches of dried basil
1 fresh bay leaf with an arrow drawn
on it pointing in an upwards direction
mortar and pestle
glass jar or bottle
30 ml (1 fl oz) almond oil
9 drops of patchouli essential oil
9 drops of cedarwood essential oil
3 gold-coloured coins
1 clear citrine crystal

1. Blend all of the herbs with intent in a mortar and pestle.
2. Add the herb mixture to the jar or bottle, then add the essential oils and the gold coins and crystal. Blend everything in a clockwise direction.
3. Hold your hands over the jar or bottle and repeat your intentions for this oil: 'I am prosperous', 'I have success', 'prosperity flows to me abundantly'. Blow your intention into your potion and seal it.

USE THIS OIL TO
ANOINT MANY
THINGS – YOUR CASH
REGISTER, THE DOOR
TO YOUR BUSINESS,
YOUR WALLET, ANY
MANIFESTATIONS
THAT YOU HAVE
WRITTEN DOWN AND
ALSO HERBAL
INCENSE BLENDS

MONEY BATH

YOU WILL NEED:

9 whole cloves
9 pinches of loose chamomile tea
3 pinches of dried basil
6 shiny gold or silver-coloured coins

This bath will help to open up the frequency you need to be in to invite money into your life. Before you have this bath, take some time to think about what is blocking you financially. Is a pattern stopping you from receiving money that needs to be acknowledged before you step into the bath? If so, write it down on a piece of paper and burn it (preferably with a black candle) before stepping into the bath. Send love and healing to the situation before you enter the water.

1. Run your bath and as it's running, add the herbs and tea.
2. When the tub is full and ready for you to get into, drop in the six coins. As you drop in each coin, state your intentions.
3. Immerse yourself in the bath and visualise the security and freedom that is coming to you with your newfound wealth.

MONEY
SMOKE

YOU WILL NEED:
pinch of dried basil
pinch of sandalwood chips
pinch of grated nutmeg
pinch of ground allspice
mortar and pestle
7 drops of ginger essential oil
1 hot charcoal disc
heatproof dish
pen and blank cheque or cheque book

1. Blend all of the herbs and spices into a powder using a mortar and pestle, blending in a clockwise direction.
2. Then add the ginger essential oil and sandalwood chips and continue to blend.
3. Light a charcoal disc in a heatproof dish (see full instructions on page 15) and place the spell pinch by pinch onto the charcoal disc.
4. Write a cheque to yourself! As the smoke travels, hold the cheque in the smoke to bless the cheque.
5. Keep the cheque in a safe place or in your wallet and expect the money to come in soon.

MONEY SMOKE
WILL CARRY YOUR
INTENTION OUT INTO
THE UNIVERSE,
WHEN WRITING A
CHEQUE TO YOURSELF,
ALWAYS WRITE IT FOR
A LITTLE MORE THAN
YOU NEED

FAST
LUCK

YOU WILL NEED:
pinch of ground cinnamon
pinch of dried mint
10 drops of patchouli essential oil
1 orange candle

Fast luck spells mean that the luck will come fast. This is great if you need something quickly or are waiting on an answer or some results.

1. Crush the cinnamon and mint together and add to the patchouli essential oil.
2. Anoint the candle with the blend in an upward motion and place it in the direction of where the sun comes up. Light it for the next three mornings at sunrise.

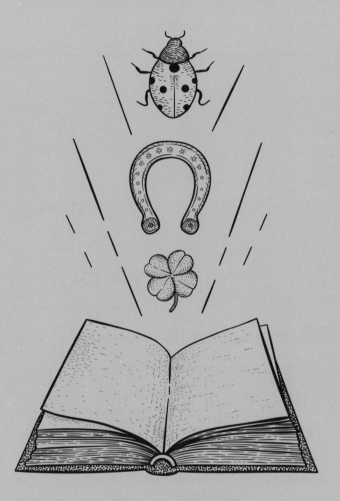

LUCK

LUCKY
OIL

YOU WILL NEED:

250 ml (9 fl oz/1 cup) almond oil
10 drops of benzoin essential oil
10 drops of myrrh essential oil
1 strip of orange peel
1 cinnamon stick
1 aventurine crystal
glass jar or bottle/plate
pen and paper/sticky label
2 green candles
2 tablespoons dried rosemary
2 tablespoons salt

---

1. Blend all of the oils, orange peel and cinnamon together in the jar or bottle, then add the adventurine crystal.
2. Write on the piece of paper 'LUCKY OIL' in big capital letters. Feel free to draw any symbols of luck. Stick this label onto the jar, place it on a plate and light the 2 green candles on either side.
3. Sprinkle rosemary and salt around the plate to protect your luck. Leave the candles burning for three nights.

USE THIS OIL TO
ANOINT ANYTHING
YOU WISH TO BRING
YOU LUCK – ANOINT
THE CORNERS OF
A LOTTERY TICKET,
PUT IT IN YOUR SHOES,
ON DOOR HANDLES
OR CRYSTALS, OR PUT
A FEW DROPS IN
YOUR BATH

OBSTACLE REMOVER

YOU WILL NEED:
pinch of cayenne pepper
pinch of ground black pepper
pinch of salt
9 drops of juniper essential oil
1 white candle

Perform this spell as the moon is getting smaller, to remove any obstacles that are in your path.

1. Blend the spices in a bowl with the salt, then add the juniper essential oil.
2. Anoint the candle in a downward motion and burn for 30 minutes every night.

BRING GOOD NEWS

YOU WILL NEED:

4 aces from a new deck of cards
225 g (1 cup) uncooked rice
1 orange candle
9 drops of patchouli essential oil
7 gold coins

This spell works when you are waiting for a decision to be made, and also if you have been a little down on your luck and could do with hearing some good news. Look for the signs from the universe during the seven days of this spell. You may notice synchronicities, such seeing certain numbers, finding white feathers... when you see these signs recognise that the magic is working and that good news is that it is making its way to you.

1. Lay down the four aces and sprinkle them with rice.
2. Anoint the candle in an upwards direction with the patchouli oil.
3. Place the coins around the rice in a circle.
4. Put the candle in the centre of the rice and burn it every night for seven days.

EXAM
LUCK

YOU WILL NEED:
1 tablespoon ground allspice
1 whole nutmeg, grated
mortar and pestle
3 pinches of cinnamon
pens that you will be using in the exam

This spell will bless the pens you will be using in an exam with luck.

1. Place the allspice and nutmeg pieces in a mortar and pestle and blend them in a clockwise direction. As you do this, visualise knowing all of the correct answers in the exam.
2. When blended to a fine powder, transfer to a dish and enchant the mixture by holding your hands over them and focusing on your future self and the feeling that you will have when you are receiving top marks in your exam. Sprinkle the mixture all over your pens and leave them to charge and soak up the magical powers of the spell overnight.

Extra power: do this spell under a full moon for super power.

A SPELL TO WISH YOUR FRIEND LUCK AND GOOD FORTUNE

YOU WILL NEED:
pinch of ground allspice
2 pinches of dragon's blood resin
pinch of sandalwood chips
hot charcoal disc
heatproof dish
image of your friend (or their full name
written three times on a piece of paper)
1 carnelian crystal

1. Blend the allspice, sandalwood chips and dragon's blood resin together. Light a charcoal disc in a heatproof dish (see full instructions on page 15). Add the blend to the charcoal disc.
2. Wave the photo and the carnelian crystal through the smoke, sending them the highest vibes possible. When the smoke stops, set the photo with the second pinch of dragon's blood and the Carnelian in the direction that the sun rises in.

You MUST ask permission before performing a spell for someone else.

SENDING OUT LUCK, LOVE AND POSITIVE VIBES TO A FRIEND IS A BEAUTIFUL THING TO DO (THE RIPPLE EFFECT OF THIS WILL MAKE YOU FEEL AMAZING TOO)

SMUDGING AND
HOUSE BLESSING

●●◐○◑

If you don't have access to a smudge stick, light dried sage or a few drops of sage essential oil over a hot charcoal disc around your house. If you are cleansing an entire house, start furthest away from the front door and work your way around all the corners of each room, always starting in the corner furthest from the front door. Finish at the door. As you move the smoke around say something like, 'I cleanse this space of all negative energy', 'Negative energy is not welcome in this space', 'Bad memories from this room are banished' and 'I am cleansing any negativity from this home'.

After a cleanse like this is the perfect time to do a blessing and fill the space that the negative energy has left behind. Burn herbs and oils over a hot charcoal disc as before, and this time start at the front door and work your way to the room furthest into the house. As you do this, you can say something like, 'I bless this space with positive energy and an abundance of peace love and joy', or 'I bless this house with prosperity, health and happiness'.

HOUSE BLESSING INCENSE BLENDS

AN ABUNDANCE OF LOVE

YOU WILL NEED:
2 big pinches of dried rose petals
pinch of sandalwood
9 drops of patchouli essential oil

FOR PROSPERITY AND PROTECTIONS

YOU WILL NEED:
1 big pinch of lavender
1 small pinch of rosemary
pinch of dried basil
9 drops of cedarwood essential oil

BATH BLENDS FOR LUCK

Light some candles, place your crystals in the bath,
add two big handfuls (64 g/½ cup) of sea salt, Himalayan
salt or Epsom salts, plus any of the following:

FOR PEACE AND HAPPINESS USE:
5 drops of lavender essential oil
5 drops of patchouli essential oil
clear quartz crystals, rose quartz and amethyst

FOR LOVING VIBRATIONS USE:
5 drops of rose essential oil
3 drops of frankincense essential oil
dried or fresh rose petals (optional)
rose quartz crystals

FOR HAPPINESS AND SUCCESS USE:
5 drops of benzoin essential oil
5 drops of bergamot essential oil
citrine crystal (hold onto this and visualise the
success you will have achieved in a year from now)

FOR GROUNDING:
5 drops of lavender essential oil
5 drops of cedarwood essential oil

TAKING TIME
TO HONOUR
YOURSELF IS
THE PERFECT
WAY TO RELAX
AND ACTIVATE
SPIRITUAL
VIBRATIONS

GLOSSARY OF HERBS

ALL SPICE
Good fortune, money, healing, uplifting. Gives extra power and good energy to any spells.

BASIL
Peace, happiness, money, personal wealth, luck, protection, blessing.

BAY LEAVES
Protection, good fortune, psychic awareness, brings positive change, magical power to spells. A powerful messenger when spells and sigils are written on them.

BENZOIN
Purification, eases stressful situations, banishes anger, adds speed and a bit of oomph to spells, good for when picking a tarot or angel card. Boosts energy and focus.

BERGAMOT
Brings happiness, luck, assertiveness, courage and motivation

CARDAMOM
Brings courage and luck, lucky for new, road opener, grounding

CAYENNE PEPPER
Remove obstacles and blockages, road opener, brings opportunity and speeds things up.

CEDAR
Personal success, wealth, healing, wisdom and balance.

CHAMOMILE
Money, success, luck, new beginnings, love.

CINNAMON
A positive blessing for yourself and your home, love, passion, prosperity, personal strength and psychic awareness.

CLOVES
Luck, courage, self-belief, personal growth, lust.

CUMIN
Healing, protection, love, lust, breaking hexes, new beginnings and emotional strength.

DAMIANA
Aphrodisiac and heart opener when brewed.

Opens the psychic portals when burnt.

DRAGONS BLOOD
Super power good fortune, grants wishes, increases potency and luck drawing to any spell.

EUCALYPTUS
Purification, cleansing, clears negative psychic energy, healing and protection.

FENNEL
Courage, protection, aphrodisiac, reverses hexes and negative spells.

FRANKINCENSE
An offering to spirits, spiritual cleansing, consecrating magical tools.

GALANGAL
Assists you to take action and provides psychical energy to help you get up and go.(so careful if you burn at night), mental power, assists with communication and willpower. Can assist with psychic visions.

GINGER
Romance, prosperity,

passion, power, can be used to speed up spells.

JUNIPER BERRIES
Magical power, protection, control, ending negative and stressful situations.

LAVENDER
Happiness, strength for relationships, psychic awareness, inner strength, psychic power, peace, meditation.

LEMON
New beginnings, cuts hexes, cleansing.

LEMONGRASS
Road opener, breaks down creative blocks and inspires creativity, brings good luck in communication.

MARJORAM
Protection, psychic awakenings, attracts love.

MUGWORT
Drink for astral projection, protection, third-eye awakening, to help you focus while making spells.

MYRHH
Psychic vibrations, offering to spirits,

protection, blessing healing. Increases power of any healing spell.

NUTMEG
Prosperity, good fortune, love, psychic power.

ORRIS ROOT
Assists with personal power and success. Communication with loved ones and work colleagues, also used to invite a lover in to your life.

PATCHOULI
Works as a magnet for good things to come to you. Prosperity, love, fertility.

PEPPERMINT
New beginnings, personal renewal, psychic protection, release, healing, decision making.

ROSE
Love, romance, friendship, lust, peace, happiness, relaxing, self care.

ROSEMARY
Protection, purification, healing, mental power, connect to your intuition and third eye, good health, healing.

SAGE
Healing, purification, cleansing, banishing negative energy, spiritual health.

SANDALWOOD
Healing, awakening psychic ability, luck, success, an offering to the spirits, powerful in moon related spells, The smoke of sandalwood carries your intentions and manifestations out to the universe.

STAR ANISE
Psychic awareness, third eye opener, astral projection, luck, keeps away evil.

THYME
Strength, courage, wisdom. Connects you to connect and trust your inner voice. Attracts loyalty and friendship.

VETIVER
Peace of mind, overcoming fear, breaking hexes, banish negativity.

YARROW
Psychic awareness, banishes negativity, faithfulness in love, peace and diffuses anxiety.

ABOUT THE AUTHOR

ABOUT THE ILLUSTRATOR

Semra Haksever was a fashion stylist for over a decade before becoming a bohemian entrepreneur and starting Mama Moon, a bespoke collection of magical scented candles and potions. Semra hosts spell making workshops and moon manifesting ceremonies teaching people how to empower themselves and feel good with the help of a little magic.

She has practised reiki, crystal therapy and moon rituals for over 20 years, and has always held the desire to create ritualistic tools that are accessible to all. This is her first book.

MAMAMOONCANDLES.COM

Nes Vuckovic is a Bosnian-born, Chicago-based illustrator and visual artist focused primarily on clean linework, surreal juxtaposition and the female form.

Self-appointed pastel queen, her work often reverts back to her blackwork roots, having primarily focused on cartooning and graphic novels in her formal arts education.

She's a B-Horror movie, taxidermy and sci-fi enthusiast. Pitbull lover. Overly dramatic Lifetime movie, wine and cheese fanatic.

ACKNOWLEDGEMENTS
AND DEDICATIONS

I dedicate this book to all of the special, amazing, caring and magical friends that I have in my life. Thank you for sharing all the highs, the lows and all of the 'aha' moments that have led and inspired me to be able to make magic and spreading cosmic vibes my full-time job!

A super special shout out to Cairine AKA Ma and Suwindi you are my soul sisters from many lifetimes ago, you both make me feel warm, fuzzy and totally supported, always.

My Chronics, Ayalah and GC for always encouraging me and having my back.

Also big shout going out to this magical lot, Tarik, Anna, Alex, Jackson, Sam, Debs, The OMOS.

Lots of love to my mum who has always told me I can do whatever I want to do, and a special mention to my fur baby Dandy, who has been sat beside me purring very loudly while I have been writing this book. I love you all so much XXX.

And, thank you to Kate at Hardie Grant for tuning in to my manifestation frequency and asking me if I wanted to do a book. And to the rest of the team: Molly, Claire and Nes.

INDEX

Published in 2018 by Hardie Grant Books,
an imprint of Hardie Grant Publishing

Hardie Grant Books (London)
5th & 6th Floors
52–54 Southwark Street
London SE1 1UN

Hardie Grant Books (Melbourne)
Building 1, 658 Church Street
Richmond, Victoria 3121

hardiegrantbooks.com

British Library Cataloguing-in-
Publication Data. A catalogue record
for this book is available from the
British Library.

Everyday Magic by Semra Haksever

ISBN: 9781784881924

Publisher: Kate Pollard
Senior Editor: Molly Ahuja
Publishing Assistant: Eila Purvis
Design: Claire Warner Studio
Illustration: Nes Vuckovic
Editor: Helena Caldon
Proofreader: Amy Christian
Indexer: Cathy Heath

Colour Reproduction by p2d
Printed and bound in China by
Leo Paper Group